Alcaeu

Poems & Fragments

Translated by R J Dent

Circaidy Gregory Press

Copyright Information and acknowledgements

Cover picture of Alcaeus: a detail from Sappho and Alcaeus by Sir Lawrence Alma-Tadema (1836-1912) Anglo-Dutch, 1881, oil on panel. Photo © The Walters Art Museum, Baltimore.

The Greek text used is from Greek Lyric 1: Sappho and Alcaeus. Ed. David A. Campbell. Loeb Classical Library, Harvard University Press, 2002

Some of these poems have appeared in issue 56 of the Acumen Literary Journal

Printed in the UK
by MPG Books Group

Paperback ISBN 978-1-906451-53-0
Ebook ISBN 978-1-906451-54-7

Published by Circaidy Gregory Press
Creative Media Centre,
45 Robertson St, Hastings,
Sussex TN34 1HL

www.circaidygregory.co.uk
Independent Books for Independent Readers

for Lauren

R J Dent

R J Dent is a poet, novelist, translator, essayist and short story writer. His published works include a novel, **Myth**, and a Gothic novella, **Deliverance**. His translations include English versions of Le Comte de Lautréamont's **The Songs of Maldoror**; Charles Baudelaire's **The Flowers of Evil & Artificial Paradise**; and Alcaeus's **Poems & Fragments**. He is also the author of a poetry collection, **Moonstone Silhouettes**, and various stories, articles, essays, poems, published in a wide range of magazines, periodicals and journals, including *Orbis, Philosophy Now, Acumen* and *Writer's Muse*.

R J Dent's Amazon page can be found at:
http://www.amazon.co.uk/R.-J.-Dent

Follow R J Dent's work on:

blog:
http://rjdent.wordpress.com/

twitter:
http://twitter.com/#!/RJDent

facebook:
http://www.facebook.com/pages/R-J-Dent/344369095423?v=wall

youtube:
http://www.youtube.com/user/rjdent69?feature=mhum#p/a/u/0/ CmnYHWJqQK4

Details of R J Dent's other works – novels, novellas, translations, stories, poems, essays and songs – are available on

www.rjdent.com

Contents

Contents

An introduction to Alcaeus

The Greek lyric poet, Alcaeus, was born into an aristocratic family circa 625BCE, and lived in Mytilene, the largest city on the Greek island of Lesbos.

During his lifetime, his country and his city were going through a time of violent transition. By 600BCE, the country was under the influence of a new political concept and practice – democracy – and the land-owning aristocratic warrior class, which had formerly exercised complete control over Greece, was being replaced.

Throughout Alcaeus's lifetime, aristocratic families struggled for political power. In Mytilene, the ruling family, the Penthilidae, were constantly fighting to retain their power against the Polyanactidae and the Cleanactidae, who were just two of the more powerful families fighting to rule.

As these familial feuds raged, opportunistic tyrants invariably took advantage of the chaos and seized control of the city-states, until they in turn were overthrown and replaced.

In 609BCE, while Alcaeus was still a youngster, the Mytilene tyrant Melanchrus was overthrown. Melanchrus was replaced by another tyrant, Myrsilus.

In 606BCE, the various Mytilene factions put aside their political enmity and united in order to fight under Pittacus, against the Athenian colonists of Sigeum, near Troy. During the fighting, the Athenian commander, Phyrnon, was killed by Pittacus, in single combat. During this time, Alcaeus and Pittacus became friends.

In 604BCE, Alcaeus's brother, Antimenidas, returned home from mercenary service in King Nebuchadnezzar's Babylonian army that had campaigned against, and eventually destroyed, Ascalon.

Around 600BCE, Alcaeus and his family attempted to overthrow the regime of Myrsilus, the tyrant who had succeeded Menalcrus.

Alcaeus had been promised help by Pittacus, but at the last moment, Pittacus went over to Myrsilus's side and betrayed his fellow conspirators.

Myrsilus and Pittacus agreed to share power and Alcaeus was expelled from Mytilene. He spent his exile near a sanctuary on Hera. He also spent some time in Egypt, and then returned to Lesbos.

In 590BCE, Myrsilus died. Alcaeus was overjoyed and returned to Mytilene. To his dismay, Pittacus was elected to rule Mytilene for ten years, and did not relinquish his power until 580BC.

During this time, Alcaeus was very critical of Pittacus's rule. Despite this, Pittacus and Alcaeus were reconciled and Alcaeus lived out the rest of his days in Mytilene. The date of his death is unknown.

Alcaeus's poems and fragments are lyrical songs, most of which are monodies, written to be accompanied by the music of a lyre. Many of these poems and fragments are concerned with the politics of the time, in which Alcaeus is clearly involved. He also writes about contemporary personalities, as well as love songs, drinking songs and hymns to various gods.

Poems

Oh, although blameworthy
I shall suffer.
Although all perishes,
I prevail.

As he had crazed wits
at the hands of the blessed gods
and was not at all well, it was best
to let him cheerfully marry.

For having been chosen, he married
and had her protected by a bodyguard
who guarded her sweetly, not letting them
toil or strive after shameful things.

He is a king to have such a bride.
Oh, that it might then happen to me
when, after much diligent searching,
I am able to find a woman like that

and eventually accept marriage.

This wave in turn comes after the previous one
and it will cause us much trouble to bale out
when it floods the ship.

Let us reinforce the ship as quickly as possible
and let us race into a safe harbour
and let no fear grip any of us,

For a great challenge stands clear before us.
Remember the previous wave,
now let every man show himself resolute,

And let us not disgrace our noble fathers
those who named our city
and are now lying beneath the earth.

Remember, we came from those fathers,
our spirit is like theirs
and we have their swift hearts.

Like them, let us confront tyranny
and let us not accept defeat.

Oh, ignorance is not all.
In spite of being a brave man,
a Pelasgians Aeolian lord,
fell from the smooth ships,

the swift ships of Crisa,
and was seen throwing out his arms for help.
He was Phalanthus,
and he was rescued by a dolphin.

Me, wretched woman, me,
sharing in all the misery
of this house,

sharing its shameful destiny,
for an incurable malady
has come upon me,

and the bellowing of the deer
grows within the timid heart,
a maddening infatuation.

Uncover that which you
have kept covered till now.

Come to me, come hither,
unless, of course, you do
not derive benefit
from your fragrant youth.

Do this before you grow old
inside your loose robe,
a dried up version
of your former self.

At the moment, your limbs
still carry you everywhere;
a boat ready to sail,
your passion the sail.

Come over the sea from Pelop's Island,
strong sons of Zeus and Leda;
show yourself to me and be friendly,
Castor and Polydeuces,

who go across the width of the earth
and the seas on swift-footed horses
and easily rescue men from death
and its coldness,

leaping on the crest of the fitted ships
shining far away, running along rigging,
carrying light to the black ship
in the troubled night...

Castor and Polydeuces, twin rulers
walk quickly over soft grass
on foot and on horseback;
leave the lovely island of Macar
and come to the land that C– inhabits.
Ride like the hurricane to the city
and free her from city dwelling.

It is the turn of the lyre
to offer reproaches:
truth is separated
farther than ever
from truth,
and it will take
a strong man,
one who resembles
one of the gods,
to end all civil wars,
to collect money
and be resolved
to spend it wisely
and not pour it away
on flowery nothings.

Such is the world
that I can no longer
bear to say prayers,
for I am sick
of speaking
to the gods
who choose to
do nothing
but as they wish.

Drink and get drunk, Melanippus, with me.
Why do you suppose that when you have crossed

the great river of eddying Acheron
you will see the sun's pure light again?

Come, do not aim at great things
why, king Sisyphus, son of Acolus, wisest of men,

supposed that he was like a god,
but despite his cunning,

he crossed Acheron twice at fate's command
and king Zeus, son of Cronus, devised a labour

for him beneath the black earth.
Come, do not hope for these things

now if ever; while we are young it is apt
to endure whatever we arc destined to suffer.

The north wind
blows through the city;
beneath the roof
a lyre shares its notes.

13

Persuasions will not work.
This is the time of life
when old age causes me
to forget all that I once knew,
all that is delightful and tender.

This is a hymn to you,
Dionysus, god of wine,
from a slight citizen
who knows no longer
what he's fated for.

Men are born – a man is wise
and has shrewd wits
but against the will of Zeus –
no, not even hairs may move
without divine will.

Long life brings distress
that must be carried deep
if it is to be forgotten.

Man is a being
who should be
delicate, pure
and holy

you should see him
bearing wine
and a lyre
to a grove

he owns,
in a precinct
at the top
of the city

sacred to
Aphrodite
and to
women.

15

O Helen, they say that one time
a bitter cure for bitter crimes
was loosed on Troy and its children
because of you – and so Zeus then

burned Ilium with holy flame...
And in a marriage without blame,
the son of Aeacus called the blessed
forth to attend the nuptial feast

of him and his young bride – a girl
he'd taken from Nereus' hall
to Chiron's house, where he untied
the girdle of that most pure maid...

And the love of Peleus grew
and she, the best of sea-nymphs, knew
how love flowered – and in a year
she bore a son, one without fear,

a demigod, who grew up strong,
not destined for this world for long,
carefree, on chestnut mounts he'd ride...
For you, a Phrygian city died.

For the sake of winter warmth
and with the cranes flying north,
I came wearing a cloak against the chill,
trusting the ship on her maiden voyage.
Thus such coldness will be left behind;
no longer will I see or feel snow.

Having embraced evil,
he called his mother,
naming her the best Naiad,
the best of the sea nymphs
and she, clasping the knees of Zeus,
begged him to support the wrath
of her beloved son

Hebrus, you flow endlessly,
the most beautiful of rivers,
past Aenus into the dark sea,
surging through the land of Thrace

and many maidens visit you,
to bathe their lovely thighs; they are
enchanted as their gentle hands touch
your water which is like a balm.

Across the sea the warriors are to be carried;
they are the regiment that destroys
everything in the name of holy Babylon.

Ascalon will fall, its ruin enough to stir up cold death,
mixing evil from the summit of Olympia,
and good from the house of Hades.

To think that after victory, there will be garlands;
one for each of all these bodies,
for all of these destroyed selves.

Pour perfume over my head
which has suffered a great deal,
and over my grey-haired chest.

As for my guests, let them drink
the evils of the day away,
and revel in all the gods have given.

And with other men, I toast Dionysus,
but the man who does not raise his cup,
you say has lost his reason.

We who will never die enter houses
to receive a blessing, a sacrament,
and not to dip the ladle into the great jar,
so cease your toiling, hearing this from me:

Drunk, you sing of how we spare the sea,
oh – of how the frosty morning air bites,
of how standing as quickly as possible
makes us remember the names of the poles.

Taking our time, aware of our leisure,
we walk towards the city walls,
turning more cheerful and with a glad heart
for there would be need for a long drink.

Drunk, you fasten your hand on me,
so I prise it from my garments.
My pounding head puts a song in your mouth.
Come, these things are nothing to me.

I kindle a great fire and you put it out.

Pronounced a state criminal,
the shame of my dear parents,
exiled from the home of my youth
with chilling care, my hardships

have managed to implant a spirit
of recklessness within me,
one that impels me to point out
injustice and wrongdoing.

So, while many strive to have a toil free life,
I spend my time criticising tyrants,
and so the spirit of subversion
was quickly established within me.

Now all I can do is calmly wait
for cold death to seize me.

Oh, but the word
has charmed many,
whatever they may say
in our fair city

He was not in all respects
unattractive nor unintelligent,
but the altar of Leto's son
should have guarded against this;
that one so base-born
should be so clearly seen

He will not deceive,
he is not gentle.

He is a father deserving of stoning,
and moreover his father, the same.

He is a shameless man,
a wicked hateful object.

Father Zeus, the Lydians,
indignant at the turn of events,
gave us two thousand staters
in the hope that we
would enter the acropolis,
although they had never
received any benefit from us
and did not know us;
and with the cunning of a fox,
they predicted an easy outcome,
thinking we would not notice them.

Someone needs to say this:
the lyre, sharing in the banquet,
makes feasting with empty braggarts
merry – and it soothes them.

But let Pittacus, married into the Atridae family,
devour the city, as he did
in company with Myrsilus,
until Ares is pleased to draw us to war;

and may we forget this anger,
and let us relax from the turmoil
and the civil war that eats our hearts
which one of the Olympians has caused

among us, leading us all to ruin,
but giving Pittacus delightful glory.

You used to be a friend;
someone to invite to a kid
and pork meal, as is
the custom in these matters.

And furiously with a ladle he hit
the jar they fill with neat wine;
the one that boils by day and night
and is splashed with wine-drops.

It was the place where the custom
is to refill the jar frequently,
but he did not forget these things
when he first created the disturbance.

He stayed awake for many nights
and the jar went on ringing.
Do you, born in such a country,
have the reputation that free men

born of noble parentage have?

The whole cargo
needs to be protected,
or at least as much of it
as is possible to protect

But she says she has no wish
to fight against the rain
or to be struck by a wave
or be battered by a hidden reef

Let her in these circumstances
try to forget these things
and to enjoy being young
in the company of you all

And together with Byccis
I keep my eyes to the sea
and so we go to the next bay,
to see if any reef is showing

These noble children
are here now shown
having done a great wrong.

Their shame, their claims
of necessity, I remember,
for when still a small child,

I sat in judgement on them
and I know the reputation
of the house of Penthilus.

As it was, he overthrew
the base-born and began
to rule as a tyrant

Such a family
would not have been

endurable.
Once insolence

and greatness
in wicked men

would not have been
tolerable.

Very often we are
thrown down

and then we are
set on our feet.

Fortune
or some such thing

has been mixed
somehow.

I tied on shoes
and visited
her father,
Tartarus,
a relative by marriage –
a lump of iron.

A foreign place,
like one's native land,
is not to be feared
my brothers,
for god wishes
the base-born
to bear their burden.

35

Through folly the enemy has lost their time.
Oh, now only Zeus himself, son of Cronus,
can end this battle however he wishes.

At present, we are not greatly outnumbered
and our losses are not a tearful ordeal,
for we still have our finest men, men

who can fight for a long time without tiring,
for warlike men are a city's tower.
If he wished to have fate checked

Zeus would have let them bring in
a champion before heavy losses ensued.
Such is my prayer: Let the sun's light

shine brightly into the dark eyes
of Cleanactidas or Archeanactidas,
and make our victory honey-sweet,

or else we are lost.

With a kiss
began knowledge
and it sits where
there are mortals.

May they give garlands
of woven flowers
to your horse
to the birds from the lake
to this city
to vine-clad stones

taken from peaks
where sweet-scented
grey-green cold water
and green reeds
are always rustling
in springtime

from peaks where
the far-seen assembly
makes its way down
the rocky hillside
on which goats graze
and roses grow

Once so lovely and desirable
you slacken from your nimble
course as your resolve decays.

I now handle gourds more tender
from which good wine is poured
and what I lost is what I now gain

for I do not have you.
You gave many favours to me
and also to those coming after.

What one gives to a prostitute
might as well be thrown
into the waves of the grey sea.

I now need to persuade anyone
that does not know this: if a man
keeps company with prostitutes

these things will happen to him:
after the business, inevitably he
will suffer disgrace and misery,

accursed misery, misery's extreme.
Also he deceives his soul, which
weeps many tears.

But she will, of course,
only have tears for another man,
whoever he may be.

The cold wave carries Sisyphus
along to the river bend.

Zeus and the blessed gods
watch as you toil, calling down curses

while making yourself a ship
which you will drag down to the sea.

Who is your benefactor?
Oh say who provided you
with a guiltless god,
when that was wrong.

Why do I want to know?
Because I saved you from your folly,
so come now and pay attention to me,
stop and refrain from evil, if you can.

Your time has now passed by
and what ripe fruit there was
has been gathered,
but there is hope that the shoot,

a fine one, will bear clusters in plenty,
although it's a little late,
for I am afraid the harvesters, looking out
for ripe bunches from such a vine,

will harvest grapes that are unripe and sour.
For those who have harvested before,
you were never strong,
although you did provide welcome.

41

From his bow
the arrow destroys;

a death
more bitter than most.

"Into asphalt
I force life."

The Lesbians have built a great precinct.
It is conspicuous and to be held in common.
In it they have put the altars
of the blessed immortals,

devoting it to Zeus, god of Suppliants,
and you, Hera, the Aeolian, Glorious Goddess, Mother of all.
One third they have devoted to Kemelios,
Dionysus, eater of raw flesh.

Come, gracious spirit, and hear our prayer
and rescue us from these hardships,
and from this grievous exile,
and let their avenger pursue the son of Hyrrhas,

since once we swore to never abandon
any of our comrades, but either to die
and lie clothed in earth at the hands of men
who at that time came against us,

or else kill them and rescue the people from their woes.
But Pot-Belly did not talk to their hearts;
he recklessly trampled the oaths underfoot
and greedily devours our city.

He does not do this lawfully,
but instead has found grey areas
in the many laws and statutes
that were written by Myrsilus.

I am wretchedly distressed,
for neither my friends, nor I
myself can mend this hollow
feeling in our hearts.

A daughter of this city,
like the vines on a wall,
has come to agree
to marry a tyrant.

It is possible the wedding
will take place soon.
None, except the couple,
are happy with the match.

Her father got very drunk,
poured wine down himself,
and laughed at having fallen down
at the foot of the royal wall.

I, poor wretch, live my life as a rustic,
despite longing to hear the assembly
being summoned by Agesilaidas
and the council.

I have been driven from the property
possessed by my father and my father's father,
both who have grown old among
these mutually destructive citizens.

I am now an exile at the back of beyond
and, like Onomacles,
I have settled here,
alone in the wolf thickets,

far away from the war,
for to get rid of strife against one's home
is not at all detrimental
to the precepts of the blessed gods.

Treading on the black earth
and keeping my feet out of trouble,
avoiding any meetings themselves,
I dwell where Lesbian women

with trailing robes go to and fro
being judged for beauty; and all around
echoes the marvellous sound
of the sacred yearly shout of women:

"When will the Olympian gods free me
from my many troubles?"

Land of great beauty, here
one would be very happy
to be an exile.

It has always been, as now,
like wine stored in jars;
a little too tempting.

To be weighed down
by what might be carried
by anyone of average strength
is the cause of much misery,
especially at a time like this,
when I need a clear head.

47

By the dim light of morning
we placed the corpses
on the pyres and burned them.
Smoke billowed through the clear air.

And the great hall gleams with bronze:
the whole ceiling is dressed
for the war-god with bright helmets,
down from which nod white horse-hair plumes,
adornments for men's heads.
Bright bronze greaves
hide the pegs they hang on,
defence against a strong arrow:
there are corselets of new linen
and hollow shields thrown on the floor.
Besides them are swords from Chalcis
and many belts and tunics.
These we have been unable to forget,
ever since we first undertook the task.

He is cowardly. This man
who seeks supreme power
will soon overturn the city.
Its fate is in the balance.

His ultimate aim is to subdue
and not to free the people;
those who are free will not be
for much longer.

Truly he well deserves to have
his beard plucked. To go to and fro
seen by all, is enough to turn
a fuller's mill.

He should be sprinkled with hot ashes
for going among the masses in such
a brazen way. He should be
beaten with a thong.

51

Once prosperous,
but now wretched,
I wander the world.

I am very lonely,
far from my friends
and always alone;

but since my exile
in this wretched land,
I have lived by my wits.

Immortal gods, please
end this exile.

We know that in days to come
there will be a bloody war
with the Athenians.

It will be us and our fathers
against Phrynon the tyrant,
who leads their ships.

He has set to sea well-armed.
Let us draw our swift ships up
and be ready.

Once again, dim men
of old haunt my memory:

Melanchrus, Myrsilus,
and, of course, Myton,

the young founder of
Mytilene, glorious Mytilene.

They broke through the line of us,
their bright blades flashing. A spear
sliced through the shield,

right where the boar had been
so very lovingly painted
on by my father.

Since many a man's fate is fixed,
it missed me. I raised my spear;
iron flashed in the sun.

It is almost a custom
here on the mountain
in the deep silence
to make a huge din,
a great noise.

Many have been taken
as guests to the house of Hades;
though once in the front line of battle,
their fortunes are now reversed.

You wish that you were able
to seek the blessings of the gods
with good faith and in accordance
with justice,

and not to suffer. Sacrilege!
Remember this: Zeus, son
of Cronus, himself controls
the end of all things.

The city
was never
the place
to quench
one's thirst
for the gods.

But now the daughter of Zeus
has given courage to us all
and we can give our thanks
by placing mixing bowls of gold,
and other offerings, in her temple.

May I remind you all
of these particulars:
that she has appeared
and all has gone in our favour;
it will stay so until Zeus intervenes.

Let us leave it all to him and fate;
to be afraid is pointless.

You missed the cup of battle.
You are like an ownerless cask,
the way that fate abandons you.
We come to lighten your heart.

I fail to understand
the direction of the winds:
one wave rolls in from this side,
another from that,

and we in the middle are carried along
in the company of our black ship,
much distressed in the great storm.
Bilge-water covers the mast-hold,

there are great rips in the sail
and the whole thing lets light through;
the anchors are slackening,
the rudders are useless.

Both of my feet stay tangled in the ropes:
this alone saves me;
the cargo is carried off
by the gods above…

It's like a whirling choral dance,
being on a benched ship,
for it is not better to try
to restrain the blasts of the wind.

From land one should look ahead
for a fair voyage if one can,
and if one has the skill.
But when one is on the high seas

it is necessary to stay put
in one's present plight,
for there is no way of
changing the conditions:

one must go
where the wind carries.

I'd hoped the thought of lending
your horses was not unpleasant.

You had horses for other reasons
than to have glory from adornment.

But now it is necessary to use them,
you say that they have gone.

… and excited the heart of Argive Helen in her breast;
and crazed by the Trojan man,
the deceiver of his host,

she accompanied him over the sea in his ship,
leaving in her home her child, bereft,
and her husband's bed with its rich coverlet,

for her heart had persuaded her
to yield to the love of this son
of Priam, this prince of Troy.

And Zeus, who knows how many
of his brothers the dark earth holds,
laid low on the Trojan's plain for that woman's sake,

and many chariots crashed in the dust,
and many dark-eyed warriors were trampled,
and noble Achilles rejoiced in the slaughter.

65

After the flower of soft autumn,
I heard the flowery spring coming.
Now flowery spring is here
and the cold frost thaws
all the way down to Tartaris.
Calm covers the back of the sea;
may you find safety when sailing.

It was a very foolish idea of yours
to try and appease Aphrodite,
goddess of love, but when the city perished,
thanks to king Zeus, son of Cronus,
they all died and went to the house of Hades.

Without them, no labour prospers,
But all is ruined by the tyrant.
There are no more fine things
and he mixes good with evil.
Does he not deserve to be flayed like a lion?

Holy Cyprus-born Damoanactidas,
I implore you in a fair season
at the altar I have made sacred to you.

And in the place by the lovely olive trees blown down,
I ask for many delights;
that when the gates of spring are opened,

you people the world with boys
scented with ambrosia
and girls garlanded with hyacinth.

For although I am not yet exiled,
I have raised money and am gone
from lovely Lesbos to the horizon.

I have fled having suffered much.
The wind catches and I sail
to the bottom of my sorrow.

The blood of women has been shed,
disgracing those who performed unjust deeds,
and we must put a rope on their necks
and kill them by stoning.

Truly, it would have been far better
for the Achaeans
if they had killed the man
who did the violence to the gods,

then as they sailed past Aegea
they would have found the sea calmer:
but in the temple the daughter of Priam
was embracing the statue of Athena,

that generous giver of treasures,
she was clasping its chin,
while the enemy attacked the city.
They killed Deiphobus too,

and lamentations went up from the wall
and the shouts of children filled the plain
and Ajax came in dangerous madness
to the temple of holy Pallas,

who of all the blessed gods
is the most terrible to sacrilegious mortals,
and seizing the maiden with both hands
as she stood by the holy statue,

the Locrian ravished her,
showing no fear for the daughter of Zeus,
giver of victory in war, grim-eyed;
but she, eyes blazing terribly beneath her brows,

livid with anger, darted over the wine-dark sea
and suddenly stirred up hidden stormwinds...

Penthilus, tyrant, If only there were
no war between myself and you;
no mingling of Ares between us,
and no cause of distress to our neighbours

I fear for our lives.
Whatever might happen,
it will be a tale to be told
to our grandchildren.

A dark cloud has passed
its shadow across the tower.
Whatever might happen,
let us be strong.

Greetings, ruler of Cyllene –
for it is of you I wish to sing:

you whom Maia bore
on the very mountain tops,

having lain with Zeus,
son of Cronus, king of all.

Queen Athena, warlike one,
who perhaps as ruler of Coronea,
stood in front of the temple
by the banks of the river Coralius

Zeus sends down rain,
a great storm drops from the sky
and the water channels have frozen

Shut out the storm,
pile up the fire,
mix the sweet wine generously,
and put a soft cushion under your head

This I know for certain:
if a man moves gravel, or stones
unworkable, he will most likely
get a sore head.

What are these birds
that have come from Ocean,
the limits of the earth?

Widgeon with harlequin necks
and long wings, guinea-fowl,
nightingales, eagle and cuckoo.

These are the birds that return.

Let us drink! Why do we wait for the lamps?
There is only a fraction of day left.
Friends, take down the large decorated cups.

The son of Semele and Zeus,
the son of Cronus, gave men wine
to make them forget their sorrows.

Mix one part water to two of wine,
pour it in to the brim, and let one
cup clash against another.

Wet your lungs with wine:
the star is coming round,
the season is harsh,
everything is thirsty under the heat,
the cicada sings sweetly from the leaves,
the artichoke is in flower:
women are at their most pestilential,
but men are feeble, since Sirius
parches their heads and knees...
Let us drink: the star is coming round.

And the cicada pours incessantly
its clear song from under its wings.
When flaming summer is spread abroad,
it charms with its piping.

For they say that Aristodemus
once expressed it shrewdly at Sparta:
'Money is the man, and no poor man
is good or honourable.'

Come, let someone put woven garlands
of anise about our necks,
and let them pour sweet perfume
over our chests.

Poverty is a grievous thing,
an ungovernable evil,
who with her sister Helplessness
lays low a great people.

Ajax, descendant of king Zeus,
Cronus' son, best after Achilles,
and with his helmet shot with gold,
nimble...

The warlike lady holds the named.
Truly she was gathering together
a scattered host of men,
inspiring them with traditional discipline.

... and if wine shackles his wits,
he will not need pursuing;
he bows his head low,
accusing his own heart
over and over again,
feeling sorry for what he says –
for what is gone beyond recall.

Fragments

86
According to the custom
we lounge in the halls
and listen to intricate songs

87
Gentle ambrosia,
increase my joy
and raise my spirits.

88
It is a fate you cannot deny:
you are a boy ploughing free furrows
before your beard is black.

89
And he with the flat head
treads slowly around the log,
and sends forth only progeny.

90
Ten thousand in all,
but inexpensive
to the wealthy man

91
A splendid altar
of blue enamel,
silver and gold.

92
...the most grim of gods,
whom Iris of the fair sandals bore,
having lain with golden-haired Zephyrus...

93
Now men must get drunk
and drink with all their might,
since Myrsilus has died.

94
We should not surrender our hearts to our troubles,
for we shall get nowhere by grieving, Bacchus:
the best remedy is to bring wine and get drunk.

95
They have established base-born Pittacus
as tyrant of that gutless, ill-fated city;
all of them are loud in his praise.

96
You have come to the ends of the earth
with the ivory hilt of your sword
bound with gold.

97
… and now he is master,
having moved the stone
from the holy line…

98
It remained untamed
so he killed the beast.

99
Flower of youth,
do not go to any harlot.

100
The water of Tritaea is a gift
to Castalia from the river Cephisus.

101
For the privilege of those who obtained you
shall by the will of the gods flower constantly.

102
May the immortal gods give us victory
over your house and your dishonour.

103
You will be steward for yourself
and you drain your cup sitting next to Dinnomenes.

104
If you say what you like,
you might hear what you do not like.

105
Wine, dear boy, and truth,
for wine is a peep-hole into a man.

106
I request that charming Menon be invited,
if I am to enjoy the drinking party.

107
Welcome me, the reveller, welcome me,
I beg you, I beg you.

108
Do the weapons of Dinnomenes the Tyrrhacean
still lie bright in the Myrsineon?

109
That they should fall is unbearable.

110
Ares says he could bring Hephaestus by force.

111
We learn from our fathers.

112
For my part, I find no witnesses of this.

113
I shall handle things in my own interest.

114
I fell by the hand of Cyprian Aphrodite.

115

The pure graces took you to their breast for Cronus.

116

May the son of Zeus, Cronus' child, look again.

117

They say that the Nymphs, created by aegis-bearing Zeus…

118

They might receive the jars of wine.

119

Wine drops fly from Teian cups.

120

Antandmes is the foremost city of the Legleges.

121

Child of the rock and of the grey sea.

122

The stream of narrow Xanthis reached the sea.

123

The stormless breaths of gentle winds.

124

Plant no tree earlier than the vine.

125

The bass swims on the surface.

126

Between earth and snowy heaven…

127

Come here and drink with me.

128

You made me forget my suffering.

129

It will not be easy to leave or to forget this island.

Glossary

Achaean – another name for Greek. Used by Homer.

Acheron – one of the rivers of the underworld. Also a river in southern Epirus.

Achilles – the son of Peleus and Thetis, and grandson of Aeacus. Also commander of Myrmidons during the siege of Troy.

Acolus – the father of Sisyphus.

Aeacus – the son of Zeus. Also father of Peleus, and grandfather of Achilles.

Aenus – a city in Thrace.

Aeolus – the father of Sisyphus.

Agesilaidas – a councillor of Mytilene.

Ajax – the son of Oileus, commander of the Locrian army at Troy. Known as Lesser or Little Ajax, to distinguish him from Ajax, son of Telamon, king of Salamis.

Antandmes – also Antandrus, a city of Troad.

Aphrodite – the goddess of love, daughter of Zeus and Dione, and mother of Aeneas.

Apollo – the archer god, son of Zeus and Leto, and brother of Artemis.

Archianactidas – the family and descendants of Archianax.

Ares – the god of war, son of Zeus and Hera.

Argive – another name for Greek.

Aristodemus – one of the seven sages.

Ascalon – a coastal city of Palestine.

Athena – also Pallas Athena, the goddess of wisdom, daughter of Zeus and Metis.

Atridae – a powerful Mytilene family.

Bacchus – another name for Dionysus.

Byccis – a friend of Alcaeus.

Castalia – the name of a spring at Delphi.

Castor and Polydeuces (Latin: Castor and Pollux) – the twin sons of Zeus and Leda, and brothers to Helen of Troy.

Cephisus – a river in Boeotia.

Chalcis – a city of Euboea, famous for metalwork.

Chiron – a centaur, tutor of Achilles, friend of Peleus.

Cleanactides – a powerful Mytilene family.

Corallus – a river in Boeotia.

Coronea – a city in Boeotia.

Crisa – a city near Delphi.

Cronus – the son of Uranus and father of Zeus, Hades, Poseidon, Hera and Demeter.

Cyllene – a mountain of Arcadia, the birthplace of Hermes.

Cyprus – the most easterly island of the Mediterranean.

Damoanactidas – an honorary form of address to Aphrodite.

Deiphobus – the son of Priam and Hecuba. After the death of Paris, he married Helen.

Dinnomenes – an associate of Alcaeus.

Dionysus – the god of wine and revelry, the son of Zeus and Semele.

Hades – the god of the dead, ruler of the underworld.

Hebrus – the former name of the Maritza River in Thrace.

Helen – the daughter of Zeus and Leda, wife of Menelaus, later the consort of Paris, whose abduction of her from Sparta caused the Trojan war.

Hephaestus – the lame god of fire, also the smith-god.

Hyrras – the father of Pittacus.

Iris – the goddess of the rainbow.

Leda – the wife of Tyndareus and mother of Clytemnestra; also mother by Zeus of Castor and Pollux and Helen of Troy.

Legleges – the pre-Greek people who were widely distributed throughout Greece.

Lesbians – natives of Lesbos.

Lesbos – an island off the coast of Asia Minor, south of Troy, home of Alcaeus and Sappho.

Leto's son – Apollo.

Lydia – a country occupying the centre of western Asia Minor. Its capital is Sardis.

Lydians – natives of Lydia.

Macar – the king of Lesbos.

Maia – the mother of Hermes.

Melanchrus – a tyrant of Mytilene, overthrown and superceded by Myrsilus.

Melanippus – a friend of Alcaeus.

Menon – an associate of Alcaeus.

Myrsilus – a tyrant of Mytilene, superceded by Pittacus.

Myrsineon – Myrsilieon – of Myrsilus.

Mytilene – the chief city of Lesbos, named after Myton's mother. Birthplace of Alcaeus.

Myton – the son of Poseidon and Mytelene, and founder of Mytelene city.

Naiad – water-nymphs.

Nebuchadnezzar – the king of Babylon.

Nereus – the father of Thetis.

Ocean – the great river that surrounds the world. Also the name of the god who rules it.

Olympians – the gods who dwell on Mount Olympus or Olympia.

Onomacles – a Lesbian hermit and recluse.

Pelasgians Aeolian – the Aeolians were once known as the Pelasgians.

Peleus – the father of Achilles, by Thetis.

Pelops' Island – Sipylus, a Peloponnese island belonging to Pelops, son of Tantalus.

Penthilus – the son of Orestes.

Phalanthus – the Spartan founder of Tarentum, shipwrecked on his way to Italy and rescued by a dolphin.

Phrygian city – Troy, also known as Ilium.

Pittacus – one of the seven sages, commander of the Mytilene forces against Athens and statesman of Mytilene, in Lesbos. He killed the Athenian general, Phrynon, in single combat. He was elected to rule Mytilene for ten years.

Phrynon – Athenian commander during the fight for Sigeum. Killed by Pittacus.

Semele – the mother of Dionysus.

Sirius – the dog-star.

Sisyphus – the son of Aeolus and Enarete, and founder of Corinth. When he died, he'd had no burial rituals and had to be released from Hades.

Sparta – a city of the Peloponnese.

Tartarus – an elemental deity, father of Typhon.

Teian cups – cups made in Teos, a city of west Asia Minor.

Thetis – the sea-nymph wife of Peleas and the mother of Achilles.

Thrace – a country north of the Aegean and the Hellespont.

Tritaea – a city of Phocis.

Troy – the capital city of Troad, city of Tros and the Trojans, also called Ilium.

Tyrrhacean – of Tyrrhaeus, the son of Pittacus.

Xanthis – also Xanthus, a river of Troy.

Zephyrus – the god of the West Wind.

Zeus – the king of the gods, son of Cronus and Rhea, father of the Olympians and of many mortals. Supreme governor of the universe.

Index of first lines

98

100